Dear Parent,

Moving from being a non-reader to a reader is one of the most magical transitions in life. For some children, it happens with lightening speed. For others, more slowly. Whatever your child's experience may be, the best way to encourage reading ability is to focus on the enjoyment and fun of a story.

Here are some ways to support success:

In the beginning, read the story aloud a few times, with the child at your side. Be sure to read in character, to bring the words to life.

Run your finger under the text as you read to help the child connect printed and spoken words. Before you know it, he or she will be participating in the reading.

Let the child fill in words as you read through the book, especially predictable or repeated phrases or words that complete rhymes.

If the child tries to sound out words, encourage the activity—but never force a child to struggle unduly with a word. Just say the word, let him or her repeat it, and move on.

As you read, allow your child to linger on a page as long as he or she likes, examining the pictures or discussing the story with you.

First and foremost, share in the fun and excitement of the story. Realizing that reading is fun **is** your child's first step toward becoming a reader!

For J.T.F.—
M.P.

For all who call me daughter, sister, aunt,
and best friend, and for my favorite little
dinosaur fan..."If Little Stevie Had a Dinosaur".
P.D.

If I Had a
DINOSAUR

by Mary Packard

Illustrated by Polly DeHays

If I had a dinosaur...

4

I wouldn't wait in line.

Basketball would be a snap.

Rainy days would
turn out fine.

A dinosaur would
help with chores...

and pull me
through the snow.

14

15

as well as things down low.

If I had a dinosaur,
I'd give him all my peas.

I would ride him
everywhere...

22

high above the trees,

in the city,

at the shore,

and to the town parade.

If I had a dinosaur...

I'd never be afraid!